Editor
Karen Tam Froloff

Editorial Manager
Karen J. Goldfluss, M.S. Ed.

Editor-in-Chief
Sharon Coan, M.S. Ed.

Cover Artist
Jessica Orlando

Art Coordinator
Denice Adorno

Creative Director
Elayne Roberts

Imaging
James Edward Grace

Product Manager
Phil Garcia

Acknowledgements
Word® software is © 1983–2000
Microsoft Corporation. All
rights reserved. Word is a
registered trademark of
Microsoft Corporation.

Publisher
Mary D. Smith, M.S. Ed.

How to Succeed in Geometry

Grades 5–8

Author

Charles Shields

Teacher Created Resources, Inc.
12621 Western Avenue
Garden Grove, CA 92841
www.teachercreated.com

ISBN: 978-1-57690-958-4

©2000 Teacher Created Resources, Inc.
Reprinted, 2017
Made in U.S.A.

Table of Contents

A Note to Teachers and Parents

Welcome to the "How to" math series. You have chosen one of over two dozen books designed to give your children the information and practice they need to acquire important concepts in specific areas of math. The goal of the "How to" math books is to give students an extra boost as they work toward mastery of the math skills established by the National Council of Teachers of Mathematics (NCTM) and outlined in grade-level scope and sequence guidelines.

The design of this book is intended to allow it to be used by teachers or parents for a variety of purposes and needs. Each unit contains "How to" pages and at least one practice page. The "How to" section precedes the practice pages and provides needed information such as a concept or math rule, important terms and formulas to remember, or step-by-step guidelines necessary for using the practice pages. While most "How to" pages are written for direct use by the students, they can be presented as instructional pages or direct lessons to be used by a teacher or parent prior to introducing the practice pages.

About This Book

The activities in this book will help children learn new skills or reinforce skills already learned in the following areas:

- developing concepts of lines
- developing an understanding of angles
- using models to calculate angles

- using models to calculate perimeter and area
- using models and formulas to calculate perimeter, area, and volume

Geometry has practical, real-life applications that can be seen in architecture, product design, and graphic design. With these concepts in hand, children are prepared for the next step: drafting, using software such as CAD-CAM, and other practical arts.

How to Succeed in Geometry: Grades 5–8 presents a comprehensive, step-by-step overview of these fundamental mathematical concepts with clear, simple, readable instructional activities. The 12 units in this book can be used in whole-class instruction with the teacher or by a parent assisting his or her child with the concepts and exercises.

This book also lends itself to be used by small groups doing remedial or review work on geometry or by children and small groups in earlier grades engaged in enrichment or advanced work. Finally, this book can be used in a learning center with materials specified for each unit of instruction.

If children have difficulty on a specific concept or unit in this book, review the material and allow them to redo pages that are difficult for them. Since step-by-step concept development is essential, it's best not to skip sections of the book. Even if children find a unit easy, mastering the problems will build their confidence as they approach more difficult concepts.

Make available simple manipulatives to reinforce concepts. Use tangrams, circles, rectangles, or any paper shape that can be cut up, to illustrate how some shapes are made from other shapes. Many children can grasp a numerical concept much more easily if they see it demonstrated.

How to Succeed in Geometry: Grades 5–8 is designed to match the standards of the National Council of Teachers of Mathematics (NCTM). The standards strongly support the learning of fractions, decimals, percents, and other basic processes in the context of problem solving and real-world applications. Use every opportunity to have students apply these new skills in classroom situations and at home. This practice will reinforce the value of the skill as well as the process.

This book matches a number of NCTM standards including these main topics and specific features:

Concepts of Lines

No learning about geometry can take place until children have a firm grasp of the lines and points. The first unit in this book reviews and reinforces such fundamentals as line segments, geometric figures, parallel lines, and intersecting lines.

Understanding Angles

The presentation of angles in this book relies on step-by-step illustrations of various kinds of angles and their relationships. Many students tend to think that angles are random amounts without understanding that there is an intrinsic logic as to how intersecting lines create angles in pairs. This unit is especially good for critical thinking.

Understanding Circles

Circles form the basis of understanding triangles, area, and volume. The problems involving circles in this book present fundamentals of radius, diameter, circumference, and the use of pi (π) to calculate area. These concepts are repeated a number of times in subsequent units about squares, rectangles, triangles, parallelograms, and the volume of solid objects.

Finding the Area of Geometric Shapes

The formulas for finding the areas of geometric shapes are quite simple. Each one in this book is accompanied by an example of the formula being applied. Several times, answers in the Answer Key show how a formula was applied to improve students' understanding.

Finding Volume

Calculating volume of objects is usually further than most students go in middle school. However, it is best to include this unit for the sake of extending students' grasp of advanced concepts and for those students who are ready to take the next step into solid geometry.

Other Standards

This book aligns well with other standards that focus on teaching computational skills, such as division and multiplication, within the context of measurement and geometry.

1 How to •••••• Understand the Concept of Lines and Geometry

Facts to Know

Geometry comes from two Greek words meaning "earth" and "to measure." Plane geometry is about measuring flat objects. Objects in plane geometry have two dimensions—width and length—but not depth. Later, in Unit 9, "How to Find the Volume of Solids," you will touch briefly on solid geometry, which is the measuring of objects that have all three dimensions.

In plane geometry, you need to be able to recognize the following:

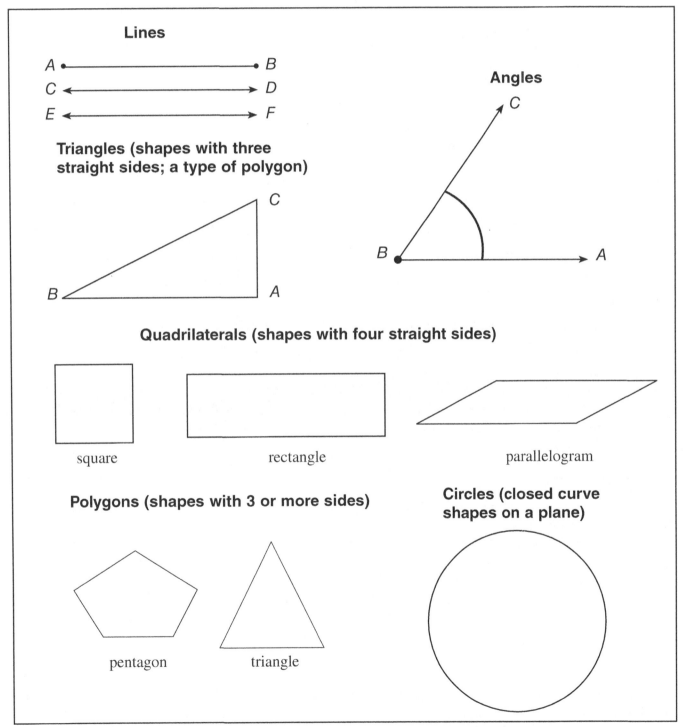

Lines

A •————————• B
C ←————————→ D
E ←————————→ F

Triangles (shapes with three straight sides; a type of polygon)

Angles

Quadrilaterals (shapes with four straight sides)

square   rectangle   parallelogram

Polygons (shapes with 3 or more sides)

pentagon   triangle

Circles (closed curve shapes on a plane)

Facts to Know (cont.)

Line Segments

In mathematics, lines never end. They continue on and on in both directions.

However, a *line segment* is a part of a line. It can be measured. The beginning and end of a line segment are *points*. Points on paper are shown as dots. Points are named by capital letters. A *ray* is part of a line that begins at a point and extends forever in one direction.

- Here is line segment *AB* or *BA*:   A •————————• B
- Here is ray *CD*:   C •————————→ D

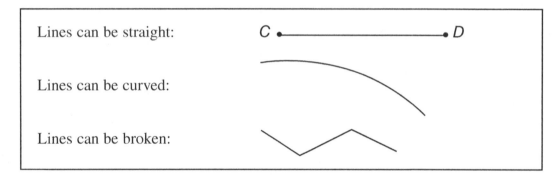

Lines can be straight:	C •————————• D
Lines can be curved:	
Lines can be broken:	

Parallel Lines

Parallel lines are lines that never meet or cross each other. Lines *EF* and *QR* are parallel.

E ←————————→ F
Q ←————————→ R

Parallel lines will never cross, even if they continue in both directions forever. Use the symbol ‖ to show that lines are parallel. Using the lines above, you would write $\overline{EF} \parallel \overline{QR}$ to mean "Line *EF* is parallel to line *QR*."

Intersecting Lines

Some lines meet or cross each other. When straight lines do meet or cross, we say they intersect. Lines *LM* and *OP* are intersecting lines.

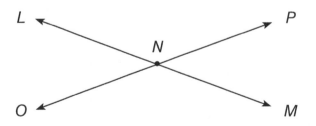

Two straight lines can intersect at one point only. Lines *LM* and *OP* intersect at point *N*. Point *N* is on both lines—it's the point of intersection.

Facts to Know

Geometry comes from two Greek words meaning "earth" and "to measure." Plane geometry is about measuring flat objects. Objects in plane geometry have two dimensions—width and length—but not depth. Later, in Unit 9, "How to Find the Volume of Solids," you will touch briefly on solid geometry, which is the measuring of objects that have all three dimensions.

In plane geometry, you need to be able to recognize the following:

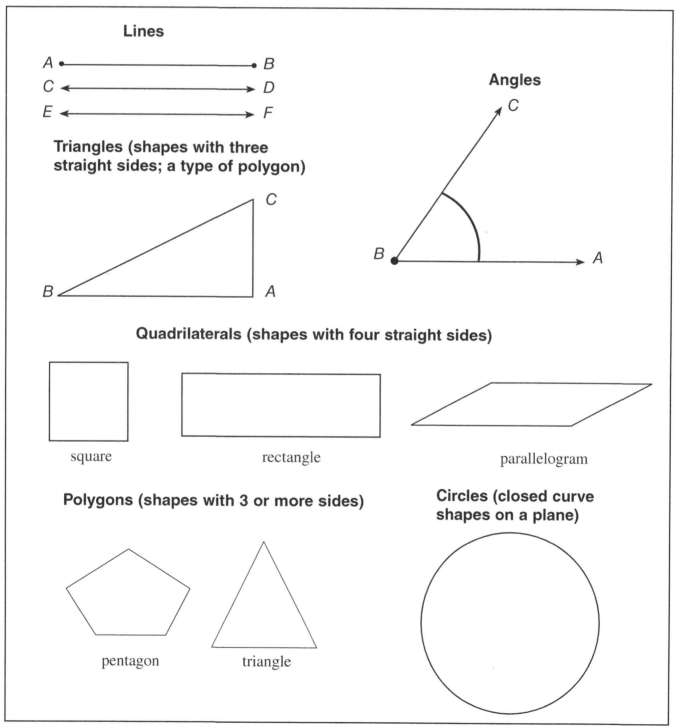

Facts to Know *(cont.)*

Line Segments

In mathematics, lines never end. They continue on and on in both directions.

However, a *line segment* is a part of a line. It can be measured. The beginning and end of a line segment are *points*. Points on paper are shown as dots. Points are named by capital letters. A *ray* is part of a line that begins at a point and extends forever in one direction.

- Here is line segment *AB* or *BA*: A •————————• B
- Here is ray *CD*: C •————————→ D

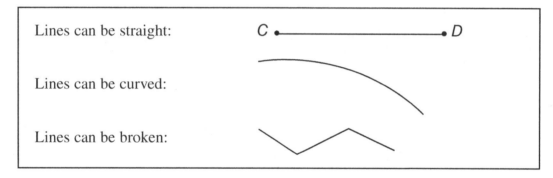

Lines can be straight: C •————————• D

Lines can be curved:

Lines can be broken:

Parallel Lines

Parallel lines are lines that never meet or cross each other. Lines *EF* and *QR* are parallel.

E ←————————→ F
Q ←————————→ R

Parallel lines will never cross, even if they continue in both directions forever. Use the symbol ‖ to show that lines are parallel. Using the lines above, you would write $\overline{EF} \parallel \overline{QR}$ to mean "Line *EF* is parallel to line *QR*."

Intersecting Lines

Some lines meet or cross each other. When straight lines do meet or cross, we say they intersect. Lines *LM* and *OP* are intersecting lines.

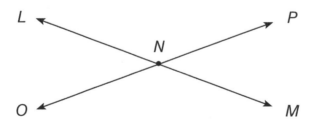

Two straight lines can intersect at one point only. Lines *LM* and *OP* intersect at point *N*. Point *N* is on both lines—it's the point of intersection.

Directions: Using the information on pages 5 and 6, choose the answer to each question.

1. *Geometry* comes from two Greek words meaning
   a. "round" and "equal."
   b. "center" and "to measure."
   c. "earth" and "center."
   d. "earth" and "to measure."

2. The difference between *plane geometry* and *solid geometry* is:
   e. one is flat and the other is round.
   f. plane is easier than solid.
   g. plane has two dimensions and solid has three.
   h. plane has three dimensions and solid has two.

3. A *quadrilateral* is a shape with
   a. sides.
   b. four straight sides.
   c. three or more sides.
   d. long sides.

4. A *polygon* is a shape with
   e. curved sides.
   f. irregular sides.
   g. four straight sides.
   h. three or more sides.

5. The beginning and end of a *line segment* are
   a. capital letters.
   b. points.
   c. line segments that never end.
   d. arrows.

6. What kind of shape is this?
   e. polygon
   f. quadrilateral
   g. regular
   h. line segment

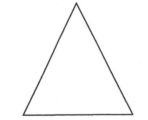

7. What kind of shape is this?
   a. triangle
   b. quadrilateral
   c. regular
   d. line segment

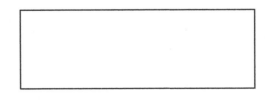

8. What is the name of this line segment?   D •————————• E
   e. *DE* or *ED*
   f. *D*
   g. *E*
   h. *D* ∥ *E*

9. What are the names of these lines?
   a. *QR* (or *RQ*) and *LM* (or *ML*)
   b. *QSR* and *LSM*
   c. *LSR* and *QSM*
   d. *Q(S)R* and *L(S)M*

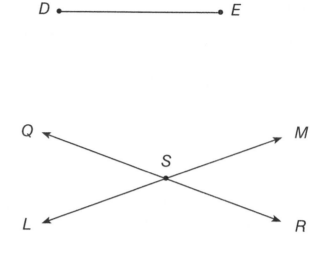

10. Two straight lines can intersect
    e. and then end.
    f. at one point only.
    g. halfway only.
    h. when they are parallel.

11. What is the point of intersection of the lines in #9?
    a. *QSR*
    b. *LSR*
    c. *S*
    d. *QR/LM (S)*

12. What is this line called?
    e. irregular
    f. polygonal
    g. broken
    h. parallel

13. What is this line called?
    a. broken
    b. irregular
    c. intersecting
    d. curved

14. Which pair of lines are parallel?
    e. *EF* ∥ *AB*
    f. *AB* ∥ *CD*
    g. *EF* ∥ *CD*
    h. *EB* ∥ *FD*

Facts to Know

Geometry is all about measuring shapes, sizes, and positions. A key form in the physical world, one that often needs to be measured, is an *angle*. When two straight lines intersect, they form an angle. You see angles everywhere in the world.

The sides of the frame form angles.

The angle below is made up of rays *CB* and *CD*.

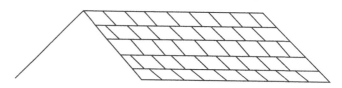

The roof is pitched (slanted)
upward at an angle.

Rays *CB* and *CD* intersect at point *C*. Point *C* is the vertex of the angle. The *vertex* is the point of intersection. Both rays of the angle have *C* in common. But what do you call the angle itself? Here's an example.

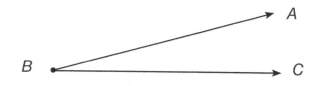

This angle is called angle *ABC* or angle *CBA*. The vertex is point *B*. The vertex is always named in the middle of the angle's name: *ABC*.

The symbol for angle is ∠. You use this symbol when you are identifying an angle. The angle above would be written ∠*ABC* or ∠*CBA*.

An angle can also be named with one lowercase letter inside the angle itself.

This angle is angle *m*.

You write ∠*m*.

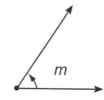

Facts to Know *(cont.)*

Measuring Angles

When you measure an angle, you don't measure the sides—you measure how far the sides are rotated from each other. The *rotation* is the curved arrow below.

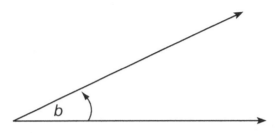

Angles are measured in *degrees*. The symbol for degree is °. A circle has 360° (360 degrees). Imagine that an angle is a slice of a circle. That slice is called an *arc*. The degrees of an angle are really the degrees in the arc of a circle.

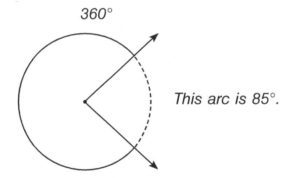

360°

This arc is 85°.

An instrument used to measure an angle is called a *protractor*. To measure an angle, line up the vertex of the angle with the circle or zero mark in the middle of the protractor. In the example below, one side lines up with the zero on the side of the scale. The other side lines up with the 60° mark. Remember, the units are called degrees, so the measure of ∠*b* is 60 degrees (60°).

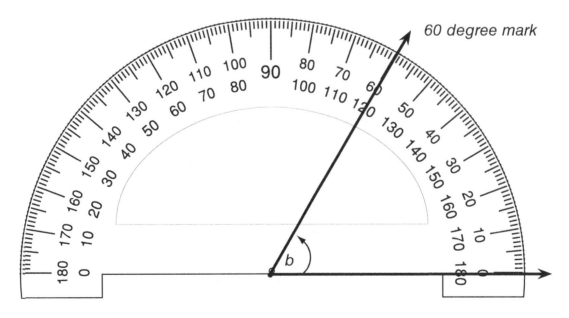

60 degree mark

Facts to Know *(cont.)*

Types of Angles

Angles are classified or named according to the degree of measurement.

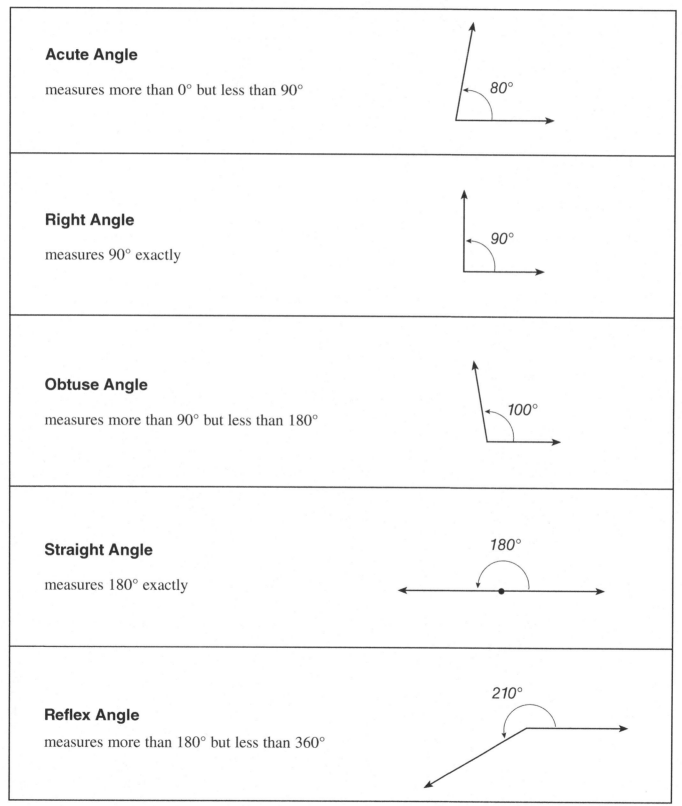

Acute Angle

measures more than 0° but less than 90°

80°

Right Angle

measures 90° exactly

90°

Obtuse Angle

measures more than 90° but less than 180°

100°

Straight Angle

measures 180° exactly

180°

Reflex Angle

measures more than 180° but less than 360°

210°

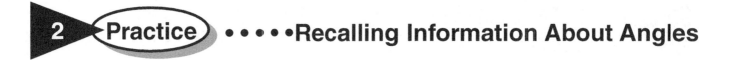

Directions: Using the information on pages 9–11, choose the correct answer to each question.

1. When two straight lines intersect, they form

   a. an arc.

   b. an angle.

   c. a degree.

   d. a curve.

2. What is B?

   e. the end point

   f. the vertex

   g. *BA* or *AB*

   h. the midpoint

3. How would you write the name of the angle in #2?

   a. ∠*ABC*

   b. ∠*BC*

   c. *BAC*

   d. *b*

4. How would you write the name of this angle?

   e. *k*

   f. ∠*k*

   g. *K*

   h. *-K-*

5. To measure an angle, you measure

   a. the length of the sides.

   b. how far the sides are rotated from each other.

   c. the circle it slices.

   d. the little curve inside the angle.

6. The degrees in an angle are really the degrees in the _____ of a circle.

   e. center

   f. side

   g. arc

   h. angle

Facts to Know

Geometry is all about measuring shapes, sizes, and positions. A key form in the physical world, one that often needs to be measured, is an *angle*. When two straight lines intersect, they form an angle. You see angles everywhere in the world.

The sides of the frame form angles.

The roof is pitched (slanted) upward at an angle.

The angle below is made up of rays *CB* and *CD*.

Rays *CB* and *CD* intersect at point *C*. Point *C* is the vertex of the angle. The *vertex* is the point of intersection. Both rays of the angle have *C* in common. But what do you call the angle itself? Here's an example.

This angle is called angle *ABC* or angle *CBA*. The vertex is point *B*. The vertex is always named in the middle of the angle's name: *ABC*.

The symbol for angle is ∠. You use this symbol when you are identifying an angle. The angle above would be written ∠*ABC* or ∠*CBA*.

An angle can also be named with one lowercase letter inside the angle itself.

This angle is angle *m*.

You write ∠*m*.

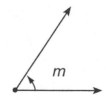

Facts to Know *(cont.)*

Measuring Angles

When you measure an angle, you don't measure the sides—you measure how far the sides are rotated from each other. The *rotation* is the curved arrow below.

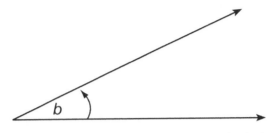

Angles are measured in *degrees*. The symbol for degree is °. A circle has 360° (360 degrees). Imagine that an angle is a slice of a circle. That slice is called an *arc*. The degrees of an angle are really the degrees in the arc of a circle.

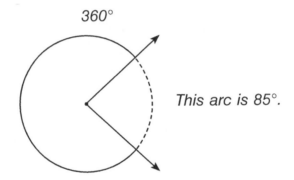

360°

This arc is 85°.

An instrument used to measure an angle is called a *protractor*. To measure an angle, line up the vertex of the angle with the circle or zero mark in the middle of the protractor. In the example below, one side lines up with the zero on the side of the scale. The other side lines up with the 60° mark. Remember, the units are called degrees, so the measure of ∠b is 60 degrees (60°).

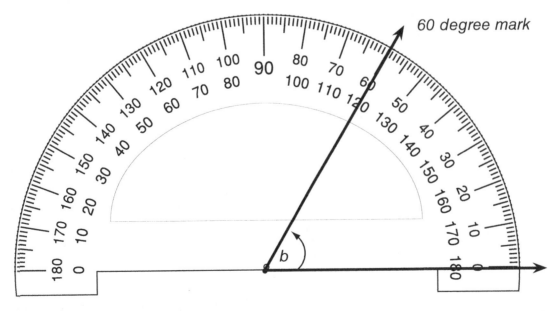

60 degree mark

7. The instrument used to measure angles is called a
   a. compass.
   b. semi-circle.
   c. ruler.
   d. protractor.

8. An angle that is exactly 90° is a(n) _____ angle.
   e. right
   f. obtuse
   g. acute
   h. reflex

9. An angle that is more than 90° but less than 180° is a(n)_____ angle.
   a. right
   b. obtuse
   c. acute
   d. reflex

10. An angle that is 180° exactly is a(n) _____ angle.
    e. straight
    f. right
    g. obtuse
    h. acute

11. An angle that is more than 180° but less than 360° is a(n)____ angle.
    a. right
    b. straight
    c. reflex
    d. obtuse

12. An angle more than 0° but less than 90° is a(n) _____ angle.
    e. straight
    f. obtuse
    g. right
    h. acute

Facts to Know

Since angles are a "slice" of a 360° circle, we can often measure an unknown angle with simple addition and subtraction.

Adjacent Angles

The word *adjacent* means "next to." Adjacent angles are next to each other—they share a common side and vertex. Recognizing adjacent angles is a key to measuring an unknown angle.

These angles are adjacent: ∠ABC and ∠CBD. They share a common side: ray CB. They have the same vertex: point B.

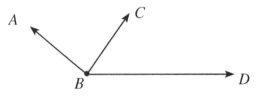

Complementary Angles

When the uncommon sides of two adjacent angles form a right angle, the adjacent angles are *complementary*. The sum of their measures is always 90°.

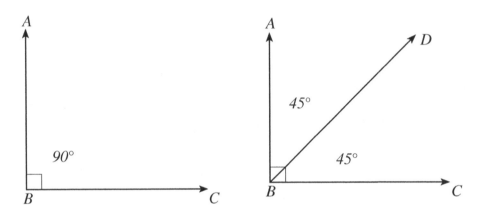

∠ABC is a right angle. A ray added at the vertex forms adjacent angles.

The vertex for ∠ABD and ∠DBC is B. The common side is ray DB. If you added the number of degrees in ∠ABD and ∠DBC, you would get a sum of 90°.

What if you didn't know the number of degrees in one of the complementary angles? Remember, the sum must equal 90°. See the example below.

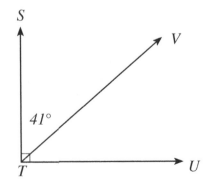

If ∠STU is a right angle (90°) and ∠STV is 41°, then the unknown angle, ∠VTU, must be the difference between 90° and 41°. Subtract to find the answer: 90 – 41 = 49.

Answer: ∠VTU is 49°.

7. The instrument used to measure angles is called a
   a. compass.
   b. semi-circle.
   c. ruler.
   d. protractor.

8. An angle that is exactly 90° is a(n) _____ angle.
   e. right
   f. obtuse
   g. acute
   h. reflex

9. An angle that is more than 90° but less than 180° is a(n)_____ angle.
   a. right
   b. obtuse
   c. acute
   d. reflex

10. An angle that is 180° exactly is a(n) _____ angle.
    e. straight
    f. right
    g. obtuse
    h. acute

11. An angle that is more than 180° but less than 360° is a(n)____ angle.
    a. right
    b. straight
    c. reflex
    d. obtuse

12. An angle more than 0° but less than 90° is a(n) _____ angle.
    e. straight
    f. obtuse
    g. right
    h. acute

3 How to • • • • • • • • • • • • Learn More About Angles

Facts to Know

Since angles are a "slice" of a 360° circle, we can often measure an unknown angle with simple addition and subtraction.

Adjacent Angles

The word *adjacent* means "next to." Adjacent angles are next to each other—they share a common side and vertex. Recognizing adjacent angles is a key to measuring an unknown angle.

These angles are adjacent: ∠*ABC* and ∠*CBD*. They share a common side: ray *CB*. They have the same vertex: point *B*.

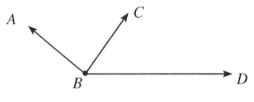

Complementary Angles

When the uncommon sides of two adjacent angles form a right angle, the adjacent angles are *complementary*. The sum of their measures is always 90°.

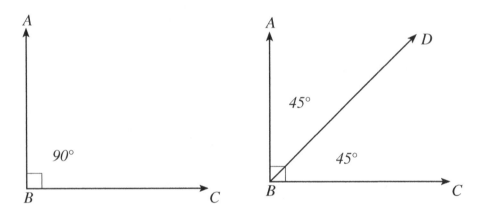

∠*ABC* is a right angle. A ray added at the vertex forms adjacent angles.

The vertex for ∠*ABD* and ∠*DBC* is *B*. The common side is ray *DB*. If you added the number of degrees in ∠*ABD* and ∠*DBC*, you would get a sum of 90°.

What if you didn't know the number of degrees in one of the complementary angles? Remember, the sum must equal 90°. See the example below.

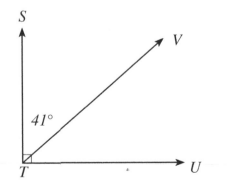

If ∠*STU* is a right angle (90°) and ∠*STV* is 41°, then the unknown angle, ∠*VTU*, must be the difference between 90° and 41°. Subtract to find the answer: 90 – 41 = 49.

Answer: ∠*VTU* is 49°.

Facts to Know *(cont.)*
Supplementary Angles

Supplementary angles are two adjacent angles whose sum is always 180°, a straight angle.

∠ABC is a straight angle.

It measures 180°.

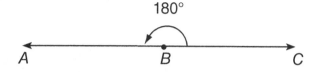

If a line is added at the vertex, adjacent angles are formed. The vertex for ∠ABD and ∠DBC is B. The common side is ray *BD*. If you added the degrees in ∠ABD and ∠DBC, the sum would be 180°, a straight angle. (See below left.)

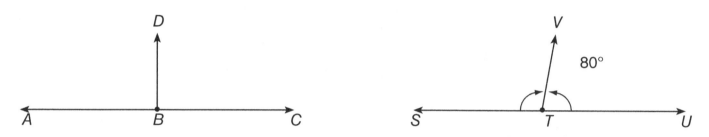

What if you didn't know the number of degrees in one of the supplementary angles? Remember, the sum must equal 180°. Figure the number of degrees in ∠STV (See above right.).

If ∠STU is a straight angle (180°) and ∠VTU is 80°, then the unknown angle, ∠STV, is the difference between 180° and 80°. *Answer:* ∠STV is 100°.

Vertical Angles

When two lines intersect, four angles are formed. The angles that are across, or opposite, from each other are called *vertical angles*. Vertical angles are equal to each other.

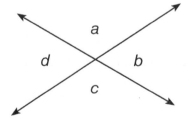

∠a and ∠c are vertical angles, so they are equal to each other.

∠d and ∠b are vertical angles, so they are equal to each other, too.

When two straight lines intersect, they make four pairs of supplementary angles.

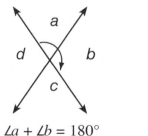

∠a + ∠b = 180°

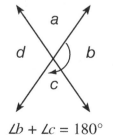

∠b + ∠c = 180°

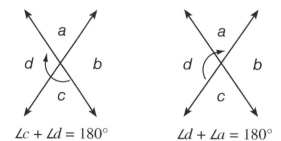

∠c + ∠d = 180°   ∠d + ∠a = 180°

Facts to Know *(cont.)*
Vertical Angles *(cont.)*

Keep in mind the four pairs of supplementary angles from the previous page. If you know the number of degrees in one angle, you can find the number of degrees in the other three angles.

Step 1: ∠*a* is 80°. ∠*a* and ∠*c* are vertical angles (they are equal). ∠*c* is 80°, too.

Step 2: ∠*a* is next to ∠*b*. They are supplementary angles (both added together equal 180°). To find ∠*b*, subtract ∠*a* from 180°. Answer: ∠*b* = 100°.

Step 3: ∠*b* and ∠*d* are vertical angles. Vertical angles are equal. If ∠*b* =100°, then ∠*d* = 100°, too.

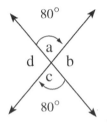

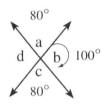

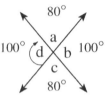

Corresponding Angles on Parallel Lines

A straight line can cut through parallel lines. A straight line that cuts through parallel lines is called a *transversal*. At each intersection, four angles are formed. The two sets of four angles correspond or match—they are identical. Corresponding angles are equal. You can use what you know about vertical angles and supplementary angles to measure unknown angles.

Suppose you know that ∠*q* = 110°. You can use this to find the measure of ∠*v*.

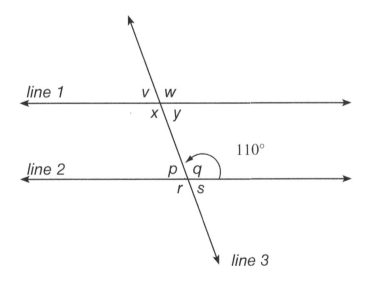

Step 1: If ∠*q* = 110°, then ∠*w* = 110° since ∠*q* and ∠*w* are corresponding angles and corresponding angles are equal. This is because *line 3* meets parallel *lines 1* and *2* at the same slant.

Step 2: ∠*v* and ∠*w* are adjacent, supplementary angles, so ∠*v* + ∠*w* = 180°. This means ∠*v* = 180° – 110°, or 70°.

Directions: Using the information on pages 14–16, find the measure of the unknown angle for each pair.

1.

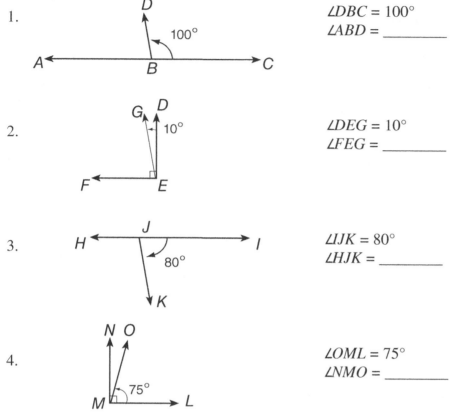

∠DBC = 100°
∠ABD = _____

2.

∠DEG = 10°
∠FEG = _____

3.

∠IJK = 80°
∠HJK = _____

4.

∠OML = 75°
∠NMO = _____

Directions: Answer the questions next to each drawing.

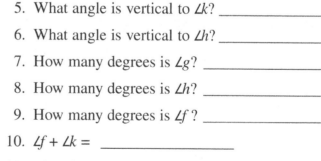

5. What angle is vertical to ∠k? _____

6. What angle is vertical to ∠h? _____

7. How many degrees is ∠g? _____

8. How many degrees is ∠h? _____

9. How many degrees is ∠f ? _____

10. ∠f + ∠k = _____

11. ∠f + ∠h + ∠g + ∠k = _____

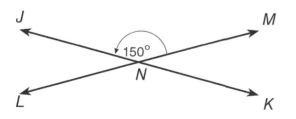

12. How many degrees are in ∠JNM's supplement? _____

13. How many degrees are in ∠JNL? _____

14. How many degrees are in ∠LNK? _____

15. How many degrees are in ∠MNK? _____

Facts to Know

A *circle* is a closed curve on a plane. All points of the circle are the same distance from the center. The length of the curve is also called the *circumference*. *Circum* means "around." There are 360 degrees in a circle.

The Names of the Parts

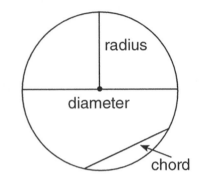

- The *radius* (r) is the distance from the center to the circle.
- The *diameter* (d) is a chord that passes through the center all the way across. It is equal to two radii.
- A *chord* is a straight line between any two points on the circumference of a circle.

Finding the Diameter or Radius

If you know the radius of a circle, you can find the diameter. You multiply the radius by two. The formula is $d = 2r$.

In this circle, the radius is 3 inches. To find the diameter, use the formula $d = 2r$.

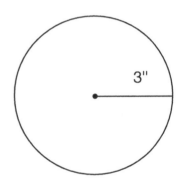

$$d = 2(3)$$
$$d = 6$$

The diameter of the circle is 6 inches.

Likewise, if you know the diameter, you can find the radius. You divide the diameter by two. The formula is $r = \dfrac{d}{2}$.

In this circle, the diameter is 8 inches.

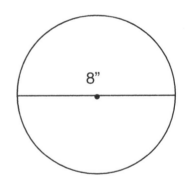

$$r = \frac{8}{2}$$
$$r = 4$$

The radius of the circle is 4 inches.

Finding the Circumference of a Circle

The distance around a circle is its circumference (*C*). Unlike some other shapes in geometry, you can't find a circle's circumference by adding the lengths of its sides—it doesn't have any! But you can find the circumference if you know the length of a diameter or a radius.

- The circumference of a circle can be found using the formula $C = \pi$ x *diameter*. The Greek letter π (called *pi*) is approximately equal to 3.14 or ($\frac{22}{7}$). On the next page are examples of problems using the formula $C = \pi$ x *d* (Circumference = 3.14 x the diameter).

Facts to Know *(cont.)*

Finding the Circumference of a Circle *(cont.)*

- Circle M has a diameter of 2 inches. Find its circumference.

  Use the formula $C = \pi \times d$.

  $C = 3.14 \times d$
  $C = 3.14 \times 2''$
  $C = 6.28$ inches

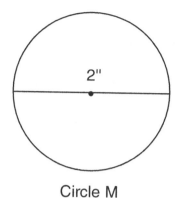

Circle M

- Circle O has a radius of $\frac{3}{4}$ inches. Find its circumference. This means the diameter is $2 \times \frac{3}{4}$ inches, or $1\frac{1}{2}$ inches. Use the formula $C = \pi \times d$. Because you have a fraction for the radius, use $\frac{22}{7}$ for π.

  $C = \frac{22}{7} \times d$

  $C = \frac{22}{7} \times 1\frac{1}{2}$

  $C = \frac{22}{7} \times \frac{3}{2}$

  $C = \frac{33}{7}$ inches (or $4\frac{5}{7}$ inches)

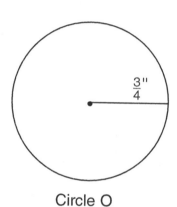

Circle O

Finding the Area of a Circle

Area is the amount of surface inside a figure. You can find the area of a circle, if you know the radius. The formula is $A = \pi r^2$ (Area = pi [π] times the radius [r] squared).

To find the area, first square the radius. (*Square* means to multiply the number by itself.) Then multiply the number times pi (3.14). The answer will be in square units: square inches, square feet, square yards, etc. Here's an example.

- Circle N has a radius of 2 miles.

  Use the formula $A = \pi r^2$.
  $A = 3.14 \, (2^2)$
  $A = 3.14 \, (4)$
  $A = 12.56$

  The area of the circle is 12.56 square miles.

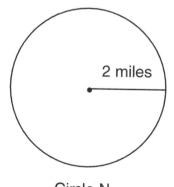

Circle N

Directions: Write the correct terms to answer these questions.

1. What is line segment *BA*?

_____

2. What is line segment *FE*?

_____

3. What is line segment *MN*?

_____

4. What is the term for distance around circle *P* called?

_____

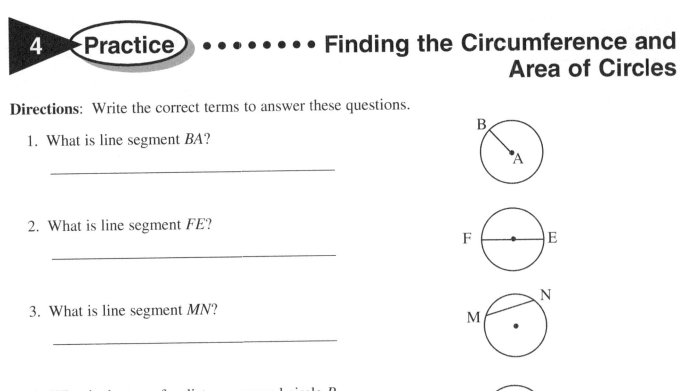

Directions: Use the formulas for finding the radius and diameter to answer these questions. (*Remember:* $r = \frac{1}{2}d$ and $d = 2r$.)

5. If a circle has a radius of 2 feet, what is its diameter? _____

6. What is the radius of this circle? _____

7. What is the diameter of this circle? _____

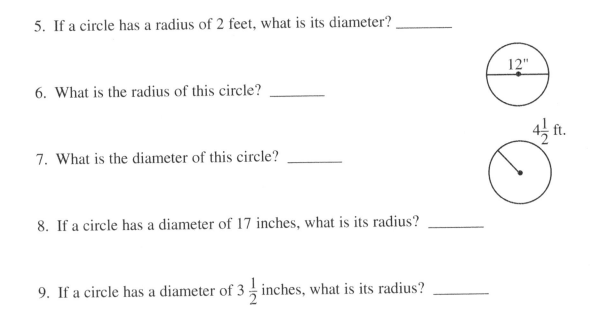

8. If a circle has a diameter of 17 inches, what is its radius? _____

9. If a circle has a diameter of $3\frac{1}{2}$ inches, what is its radius? _____

Directions: Use the formula for finding the circumference of each circle ($C = \pi \times d$, where $\pi = 3.14$ unless noted.).

10. What is the circumference of this circle? _____

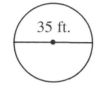

35 ft.

11. What is the circumference of this circle? _____

6.5 miles

12. What is the circumference of this circle? (Use $\pi = \frac{22}{7}$.) _____

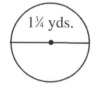

1¼ yds.

Directions: Use the formula for finding the area of these circles ($A = \pi r^2$ where $\pi = 3.14$).

13. What is the area of this circle? _____

12 ft.

14. What is the area of this circle? _____

14"

15. What is the area of this circle? _____

10'

Facts to Know

A *triangle*, in plane geometry, is a closed figure that has three line segments for sides. The sides meet at three points called *vertices*, and each *vertex* forms an angle with two of the sides. The word *triangle* means "three angles." The sum of the three angles of a triangle is always 180°.

The symbol for triangle is △. You use it when you write the name of a triangle.

A triangle is named with the letters at each angle. The triangle below could have six names: △ *BAC*, △ *CAB*, △ *ABC*, △ *BCA*, △ *CBA, or* △ *ACB*.

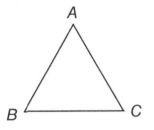

The angles are named with the letters of the sides. Look at the right-hand angle in the triangle to the left. It could be named ∠ *BCA* or ∠ *ACB*. The letter of the vertex is always in the middle of the name.

An angle in a triangle can also be named by the letter at its vertex: ∠ *C*.

You can figure out an unknown angle in a triangle if you know the measure of the other two angles. Since the sum of the angles in a triangle is always 180°, you can use addition and then subtraction to find the unknown angle. Here's an example:

∠ *KLM* = 95°

∠ *LMK* = 30°

Find ∠ *MKL*.

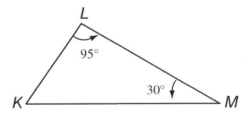

Step 1: Add the two known angles: 95° + 30° = 125°.

Step 2: The sum of the three angles is 180°. Subtract the sum of the two known angles to find the measure of ∠ *MKL*: 180° − 125° = 55°. ∠ *MKL* = 55°

Facts to Know *(cont.)*

Triangles Named by the Sizes of Their Angles

Triangles are named according to either their largest angle or the lengths of their sides. You may want to review Unit 2, "How to Understand Angles," before beginning this unit.

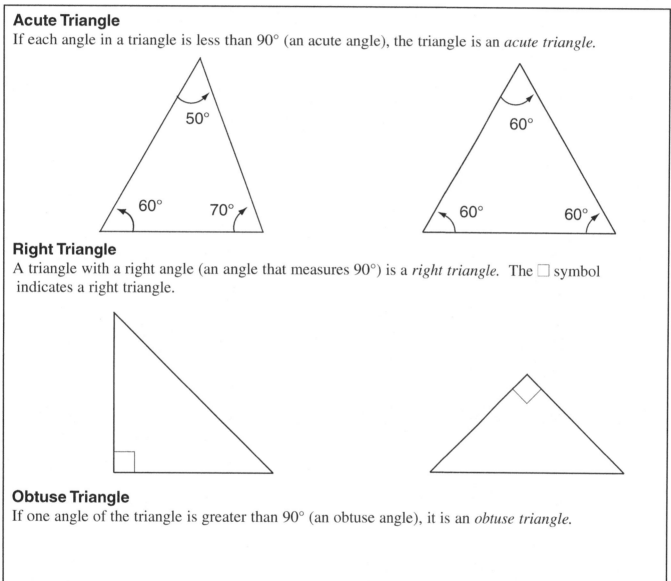

Acute Triangle

If each angle in a triangle is less than 90° (an acute angle), the triangle is an *acute triangle.*

Right Triangle

A triangle with a right angle (an angle that measures 90°) is a *right triangle.* The ☐ symbol indicates a right triangle.

Obtuse Triangle

If one angle of the triangle is greater than 90° (an obtuse angle), it is an *obtuse triangle.*

Note: No triangle can have more than one obtuse or one right angle.

Facts to Know *(cont.)*

Triangles Named by the Length of Their Sides

Equilateral Triangle

Equi means "equal" and *lateral* means "sides." An *equilateral triangle* has three sides of the same length. An equilateral triangle also has three equal angles.

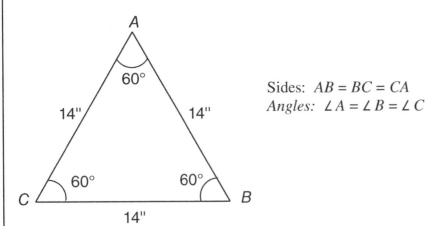

Sides: *AB = BC = CA*
Angles: ∠*A* = ∠*B* = ∠*C*

Isosceles Triangle

An *isosceles triangle* is a triangle with two equal sides. An isosceles triangle also has two equal angles because it has two equal sides. Angles that are opposite equal sides are also equal.

Side *MO* = Side *ON*

∠*M* is opposite side *ON* and ∠*N* is opposite *MO*

So, ∠*M* = ∠*N*.

Scalene Triangle

A *scalene triangle* is a triangle with no equal sides. Because there are no equal sides, there are no equal angles. All the angles have different measures.

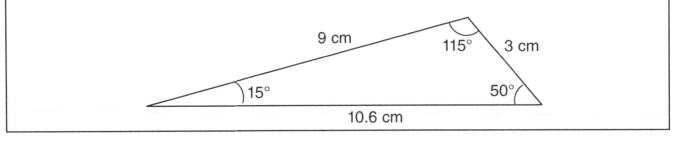

5 ▷ Practice • • • • • • • • • • • • • • • • • Identifying Triangles

Directions: Write the correct answer to each question.

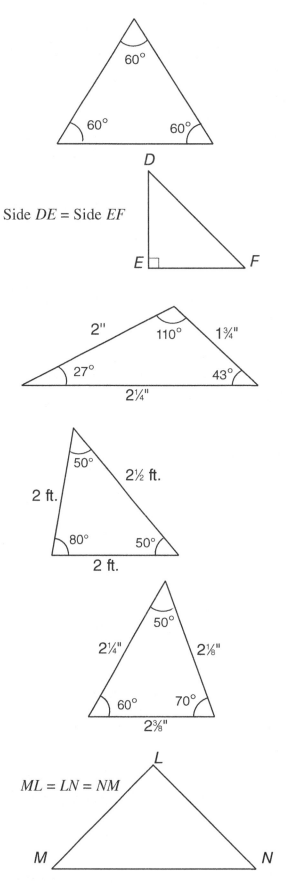

1. What is the name of this triangle by the size of its angles? _____

2. What is the name of this triangle by the length of its sides? _____

3. What is the name of this triangle by the size of its angles? _____

4. What is the name of this triangle by the length of its sides? _____

5. What is the name of this triangle by the size of its angles? _____

6. What is the name of this triangle by the length of its sides? _____

7. What is the name of this triangle by the size of its angles? _____

8. What is the name of this triangle by the length of its sides? _____

9. What is the name of this triangle by the size of its angles? _____

10. What is the name of this triangle by the length of its sides? _____

11. What is the name of this triangle by the size of its angles? _____

12. What is the name of this triangle by the length of its sides? _____

Facts to Know

Knowing the lengths of a triangle's sides can tell you something about its angles. The longest side of a triangle is the side opposite the largest angle. The shortest side is the side opposite the smallest angle.

Examining Triangles

Here are some examples showing the link between the length of a triangle's sides and its angles.

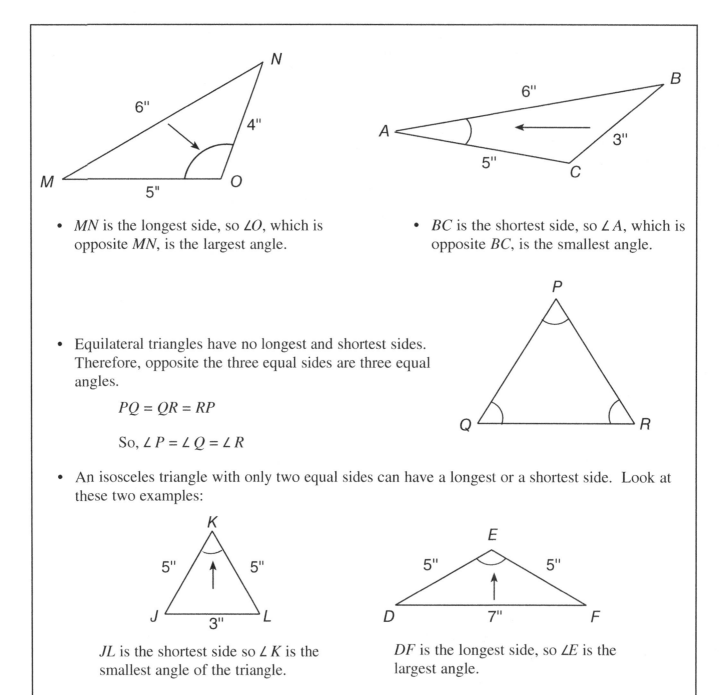

- *MN* is the longest side, so ∠*O*, which is opposite *MN*, is the largest angle.

- *BC* is the shortest side, so ∠*A*, which is opposite *BC*, is the smallest angle.

- Equilateral triangles have no longest and shortest sides. Therefore, opposite the three equal sides are three equal angles.

  PQ = QR = RP

  So, ∠*P* = ∠*Q* = ∠*R*

- An isosceles triangle with only two equal sides can have a longest or a shortest side. Look at these two examples:

JL is the shortest side so ∠*K* is the smallest angle of the triangle.

DF is the longest side, so ∠*E* is the largest angle.

The other two angles in an isosceles triangle are opposite equal sides, so they are equal. Above, ∠*J* = ∠*L* and ∠*D* = ∠*F*.

Facts to Know *(cont.)*

Examining Triangles *(cont.)*

Using the information on the previous page, you can solve problems about triangles—their type and the size of their angles. In addition, you may be able to figure out the size of two angles if one angle and the sides are given. Look at this example that uses △ DEF.

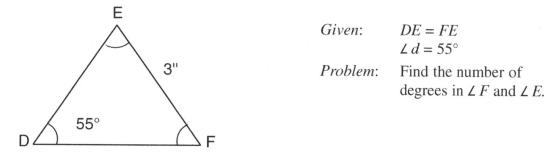

Given: $DE = FE$
             $\angle d = 55°$

Problem: Find the number of
             degrees in $\angle F$ and $\angle E$.

Step 1: Determine if there are any equal sides. Side DE = side FE, so the angles opposite these two sides are equal: $\angle D = \angle F$. Since $\angle D = 55°$, then $\angle F = 55°$, too.

Step 2: Find the number of degrees in $\angle E$. Remember, the sum of all the angles in a triangle is 180°. You know two of them now, $\angle D$ and $\angle F$, which are both 55°. Add the two angles and then subtract the sum from 180° to find $\angle E$.

$55 + 55 = 110$
$180 - 110 = 70$
So, $\angle E = 70°$.

Here's another example. This time, you don't know the lengths of the sides, but you can find the measures all three angles.

Step 1: Find the number of degrees in $\angle a$. You know that $\angle a$ and the 130° angle are supplementary, therefore, $\angle a$ + 130° = 180°. Subtract to find $\angle a$.

$\angle a = 180° - 130°$
So, $\angle a = 50°$.

Find $\angle b$.

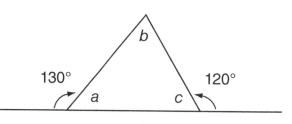

Step 2: Find $\angle c$. You know that $\angle c$ and the 120° angle are supplementary angles, therefore $\angle c + 120° = 180°$; subtract to find $\angle c$.

$\angle c = 180° - 120°$
So, $\angle c = 60°$.

Step 3: Find $\angle b$. The sum of the angles in a triangle is 180°. You know the number of degrees in two of the angles.
$\angle a + \angle c = 50° + 60° = 110°$

$\angle b = 180° - 110°$
So, $\angle b = 70°$.

Facts to Know *(cont.)*

Right Triangles and the Hypotenuse

The sides of a right triangle have a special relationship. When you add the squares of the two shortest sides, the sum equals the square of the longest side. In a right triangle, the longest side is called the *hypotenuse*. The other two sides are called *legs*.

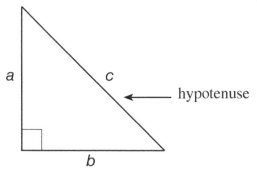 hypotenuse

The formula for finding the hypotenuse is
side a^2 + side b^2 = side c^2 (hypotenuse) or $a^2 + b^2 = c^2$.

This rule was discovered by a Greek mathematician named Pythagoras, and so the formula is called the *Pythagorean theorem* which states: "The square of the hypotenuse is equal to the sum of the squares of the other two sides."

Here's how to find the hypotenuse of a triangle.

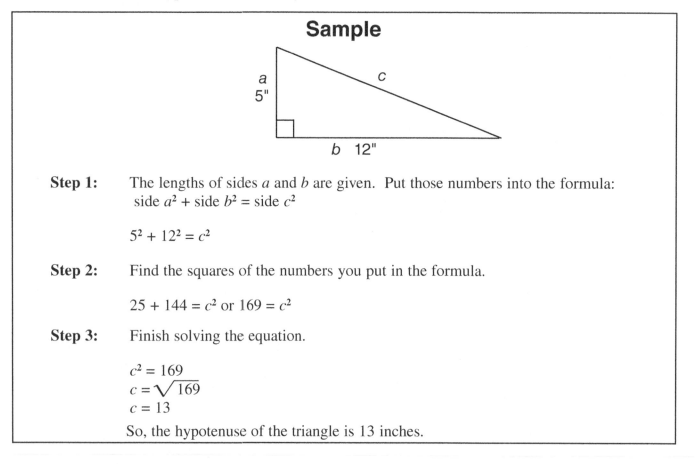

Sample

Step 1: The lengths of sides *a* and *b* are given. Put those numbers into the formula:
side a^2 + side b^2 = side c^2

$5^2 + 12^2 = c^2$

Step 2: Find the squares of the numbers you put in the formula.

$25 + 144 = c^2$ or $169 = c^2$

Step 3: Finish solving the equation.

$c^2 = 169$
$c = \sqrt{169}$
$c = 13$

So, the hypotenuse of the triangle is 13 inches.

6 ▶ Practice • • • • • • • • • Finding the Degrees of Angles in Triangles

Directions: Write the correct answer.

Given △ ABC, where ∠ A = ∠ 55° and B = ∠ 65° . . .

1. What is the measurement of ∠ C? _____

2. What kind of triangle is △ ABC? _____

Given △ DEF, where ∠ D = 60° and ∠ E = 60° . . .

3. What is the measure of ∠ F? __

4. What kind of triangle is △ DEF? _____

Given side DE (3 inches), side EF (3 inches), and ∠ E (70°) . . .

5. Find ∠ D and ∠ F. _____

Given an isosceles triangle, where ∠ m = ∠ p . . .

6. Find ∠ n. _____

7. Find the hypotenuse of this right triangle.

_____

8. Find the missing side (b) of this right triangle.

_____

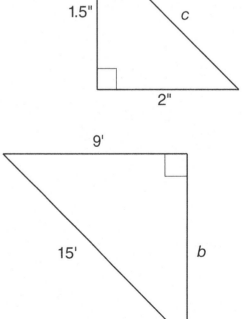

Facts to Know

A *quadrilateral* is the name given to a plane figure with four straight sides. In other words, it's a four-sided polygon. Quadrilaterals are also called *quadrangles*. Quadrangles have four straight sides and four angles.

Kinds of Quadrangles

- **Square**

  A *square* has four sides, all the same length. It has four right angles and two pairs of parallel sides.

  $\overline{AB} \parallel \overline{CD}$ and $\overline{AC} \parallel \overline{BD}$

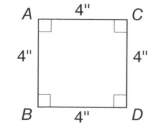

- **Rectangle**

  A *rectangle* has equal opposite sides. It has four right angles and two pairs of parallel sides.

  $\overline{EF} \parallel \overline{GH}$ and $\overline{EG} \parallel \overline{FH}$

- **Rhombus**

  A *rhombus* has four equal sides like a square. It has two pairs of parallel sides. It has equal opposite angles.

  $\overline{AB} \parallel \overline{CD}$ and $\overline{AC} \parallel \overline{BD}$

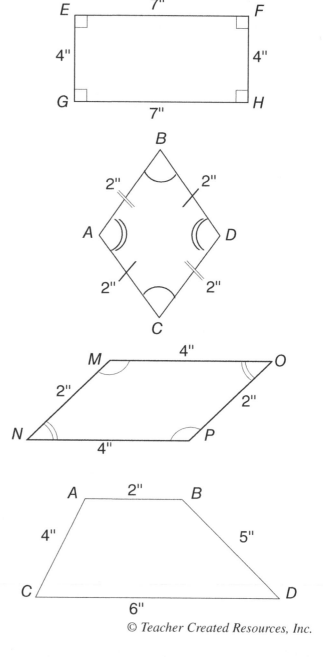

- **Parallelogram**

  A parallelogram has equal opposite sides like a rectangle. It has two pairs of parallel sides. It has equal opposite angles. A rhombus is a kind of parallelogram.

  $\overline{MO} \parallel \overline{NP}$ and $\overline{MN} \parallel \overline{OP}$

- **Trapezoid**

  A trapezoid has only one pair of parallel sides.

  $\overline{AB} \parallel \overline{CD}$

Facts to Know *(cont.)*

Finding Perimeter

Perimeter is the distance around a figure.

To find the perimeter of a triangle, a quadrilateral, or a polygon—a figure with three sides or more—you add the lengths of the sides.

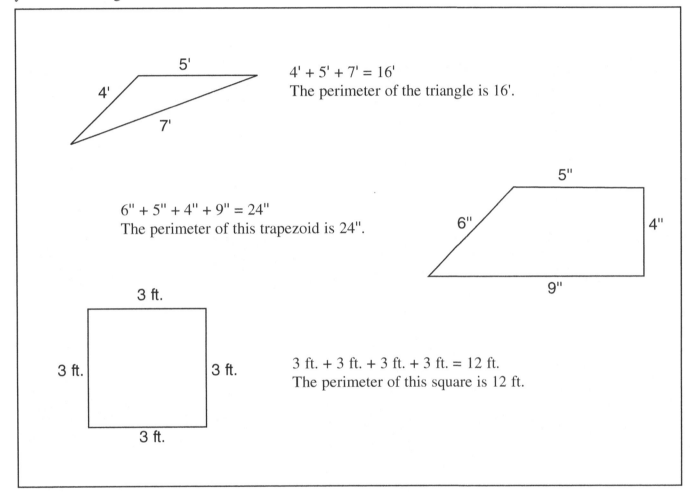

5'
4'
7'

4' + 5' + 7' = 16'
The perimeter of the triangle is 16'.

6" + 5" + 4" + 9" = 24"
The perimeter of this trapezoid is 24".

5"
6"
4"
9"

3 ft.
3 ft.
3 ft.
3 ft.

3 ft. + 3 ft. + 3 ft. + 3 ft. = 12 ft.
The perimeter of this square is 12 ft.

There are formulas for finding perimeter, but sometimes just adding up the sides is faster.

- For the perimeter of a square: *P (Perimeter)* = 4*s* (*side*). For the square above, enter the numbers in the formula, *P* = 4(3 ft.) or 12 ft.

- For the perimeter of a rectangle or parallelogram:
  P (Perimeter) = 2*w* (*width*) + 2*l* (*length*). Let's say you knew the lengths of two sides of a rectangle.

  You could use the formula:
  P = 2(5 ft.) + 2(14 ft.), which is 38 ft.

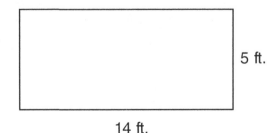

5 ft.

14 ft.

Directions: Read the clues and answer the questions.

1. It has 2 pairs of equal opposite sides like a rectangle.
   It has two pairs of parallel sides.
   It has 2 pairs of equal opposite angles.
   What kind of quadrangle is it?

   _____

2. It has one pair parallel sides.
   What kind of quadrangle is it?

   _____

Directions: Identify the following quadrangles.

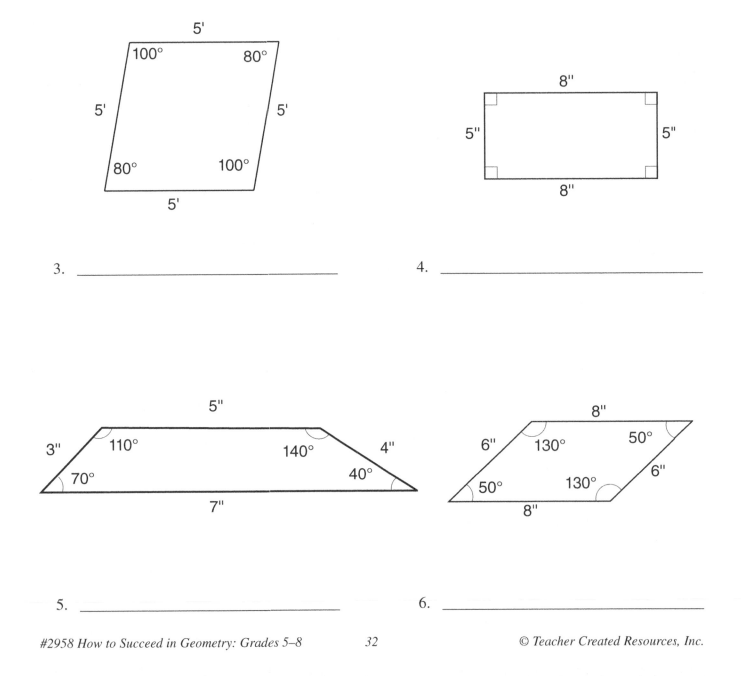

3. _____

4. _____

5. _____

6. _____

Directions: Find the perimeter.

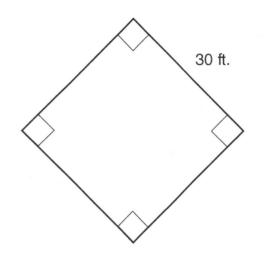

7. _____

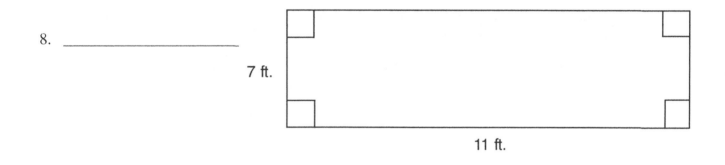

8. _____

9. A parallelogram has a perimeter of 13 feet. Its length is 3.75 feet. What is its width? _____

10. A square has a perimeter of 28 feet. What is the length of one side? _____

11. Grandma's garden has sides of 15 ft., 10 ft., 8 ft., and 12 ft.
    How much fencing does she need to keep the rabbits out? _____

12. Myra's poster of the Rockin' Jellybeans measures 4 ft. by 3 ft.
    How much frame does she need to go around it? _____

Facts to Know

Area is the amount of space on a flat surface. Area is measured in square units: square inches, square feet, square miles, etc. Think of a surface covered with square tiles. In the drawing below, each tile is 1 square inch.

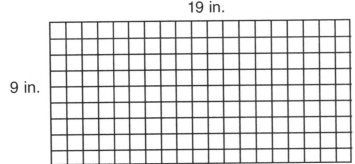

19 in.

9 in.

If you counted them all, you would find there are 171 square inches in this 19 in. by 9 in. rectangle. But there's a simpler way to arrive at the total number of square inches.

Finding the Area of Rectangles

In the rectangle above, there are 9 rows of 19 square inches. A shortcut is to multiply 9 in. x 19 in., which would give you 171 square inches.

The formula for finding the area of a rectangle is *A* (*area*) = *l* (*length*) x *w* (*width*).

Here's an example using the formula:

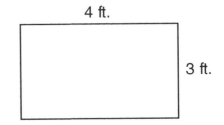

4 ft.

3 ft.

$A = l \text{ x } w$
$A = 4 \text{ ft. x } 3 \text{ ft.}$
$A = 12 \text{ ft.}^2$

So, the area is 12 sq. ft.

Always remember to add square or sq. in the answer to an area problem.

Finding the Area of Squares

A square is a quadrilateral with four equal sides. The formula to find the area is even simpler:
A (*area*) = *s* (*side*) x *s* (*side*) or *A* = *s*².

Using the formula,

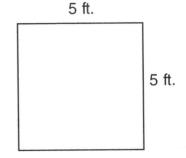

5 ft.

5 ft.

$A = s \text{ x } s$
$A = 5 \text{ ft. x } 5 \text{ ft.}$
$A = 25 \text{ ft.}^2$

So, the area of the square is 25 sq. ft.

Facts to Know *(cont.)*

Finding the Area of Triangles

To find the area of a triangle, you need to know the base and the height. The base can be any side of the triangle. The height of a triangle is its *altitude*.

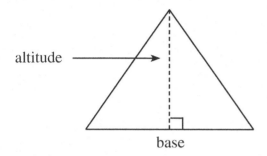

The altitude is a line that is perpendicular to the base and extends from the angle opposite the base.

Perpendicular lines form right (90°) angles.

To find the area, the height or altitude must be given so that you can put the numbers into the formula, A (*area*) $= \frac{1}{2} b$ (*base*) x h (*height*) or $A = \frac{1}{2} bh$.

Here's an example using the formula: $A = \frac{1}{2} \times 10 \times 8$

$A = \frac{1}{2} (80)$

$A = 40$

So, the area of the triangle is 40 sq. ft.

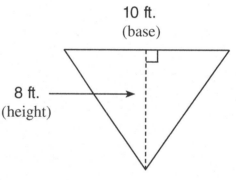

Finding the Area of Parallelograms

You use the same logic for finding the area of a triangle to find the area of a parallelogram. To find the area, the height must be given in the problem.

The formula is A (*area*) $= b$ (*base*) x h (*height*) or $A = bh$.

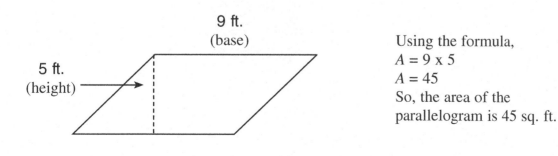

Using the formula,
$A = 9 \times 5$
$A = 45$
So, the area of the parallelogram is 45 sq. ft.

Directions: Answer the questions.

1. The high jump pit is a rectangle 12 feet long and 10 feet wide.

   What is the area? _____

2. Ingrid is purchasing a rectangular rug that measures 6 ft. by 8 ft.

   How many square feet of floor space will it cover? _____

3. A baseball field has 20 yards between bases. The Izaac Walton Ball Club wants to buy a tarp that will cover the field at night.

   How big will the tarp have to be? _____

4. What is the area of the square below? _____ What is the area of the rectangle below? _____

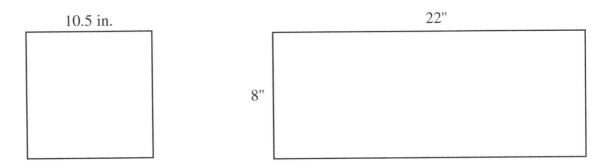

10.5 in.

22"

8"

5. Ingrid's first rug was too small. So, she bought a 8 ft. by 10 ft. rug instead. It's going to go in a 10 ft. by 12 ft. room. How much floor space won't be covered by the rug? _____

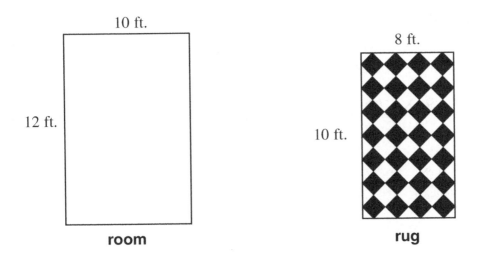

10 ft.

12 ft.

room

8 ft.

10 ft.

rug

6. Find the area of a rectangle that has a length of 6.5 ft. and a width of 2.25 ft. _____

Directions: Find the area of each triangle.

7.

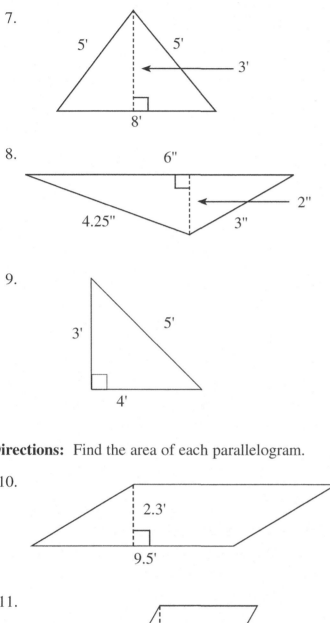

Area = _____

8.

Area = _____

9.

Area = _____

Directions: Find the area of each parallelogram.

10.

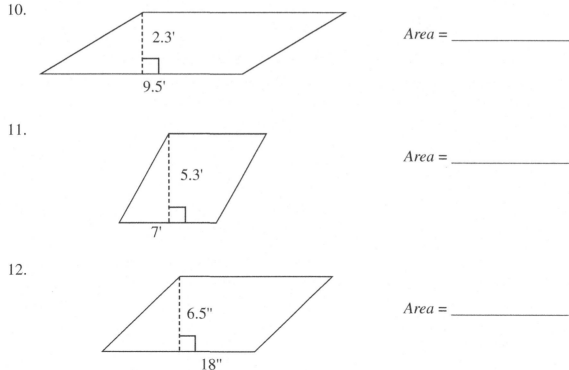

Area = _____

11.

Area = _____

12.

Area = _____

Facts to Know

Plane geometry involves measuring flat or two-dimensional figures. *Solid geometry* is measuring figures with three, instead of two, dimensions—length, width, and height.

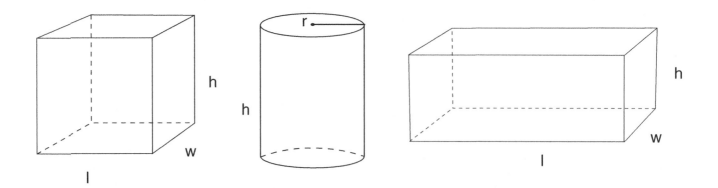

One way to measure how much an object can hold is to measure its *volume*. The unit used to measure volume is a cube. The *cube* may be 1 cm on each side (a cubic centimeter), 1 in. on each side (a cubic inch), 1 ft. on each side (a cubic foot), etc.

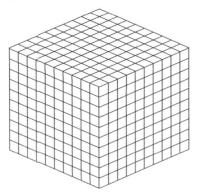

Imagine that each one of the small squares is a cubic inch. Adding them all up would give you the volume in cubic inches of this cube.

Finding the Volume of Rectangular Solids

To find the volume of a rectangular solid, use the formula *Volume = l (length) x w (width) x h (height)* or *V = lwh*. So volume is simply the area of the base rectangle times the height.

Here's an example:

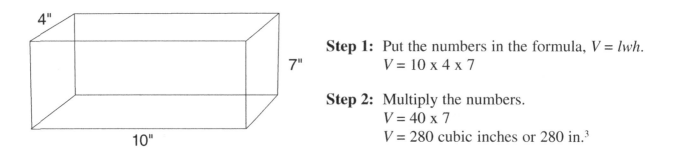

Step 1: Put the numbers in the formula, *V = lwh*.
$V = 10 \times 4 \times 7$

Step 2: Multiply the numbers.
$V = 40 \times 7$
$V = 280$ cubic inches or 280 in.^{3}

Facts to Know *(cont.)*

Finding the Volume of Cubes

A cube has six equal sides. The length, width, and height are all equal. The formula for finding the volume of a cube is s^3 (*side* x *side* x *side*). Another way of looking at it is s^3 is really the area of the *base* (s^2) x the *height* (s).

Here's an example:

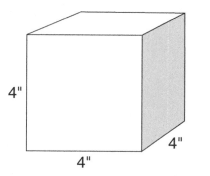

Step 1: Put the numbers in the formula, $V = s^3$.
$$V = 4^3$$
$$V = 4 \times 4 \times 4$$

Step 2: Multiply the numbers.
$$V = 16 \,(4)$$
So, $V = 64$ cubic inches or 64 in.^{3}

Finding the Volume of Cylinders

The top and bottom of a cylinder are circles, but the side of the cylinder "unrolls" or flattens out into a rectangle.

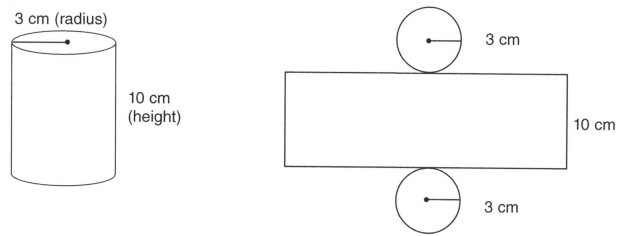

The formula for finding the volume of a cylinder is $V = \pi$ (pi) x r (*radius squared*) x h (*height*) or $V = \pi\, r^2 h$. Find the volume of the cylinder above. (Remember that π is roughly equal to 3.14.)

Step 1: Put the numbers in the formula: $V = \pi\, r^2\, h$.
$$V = 3.14 \times 3^2 \times 10$$
$$V = 3.14 \times 9 \times 10$$

Step 2: Multiply the numbers.
$$V = 28.26 \times 10$$
So, $V = 282.6$ cubic centimeters or 282.6 cm^3.

9 ►Practice ••••••••• Finding the Volumes of Solids

Directions: Use the formulae in this unit to answer the questions.

1. What is the volume of this rectangular solid?

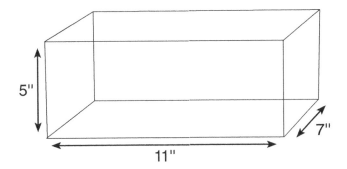

Volume = _____

2. What is the volume of this cube?

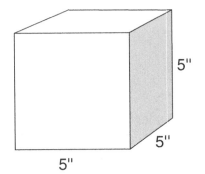

Volume = _____

3. What is the volume of this cylinder? (Round to the nearest inch.)

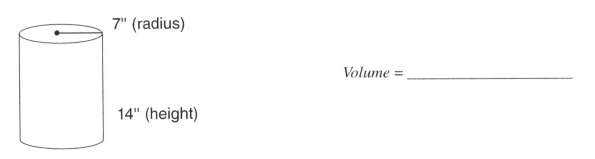

7" (radius)

14" (height)

Volume = _____

4. What is the volume of this cylinder? (Round to the nearest inch.)

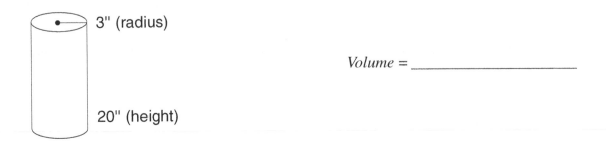

3" (radius)

20" (height)

Volume = _____

5. The sidewalk leading up to the school needs to be replaced. It has to be 4' wide, 100' long, and 1' deep. How much concrete should be poured? _____

6. What is the volume of this cube?

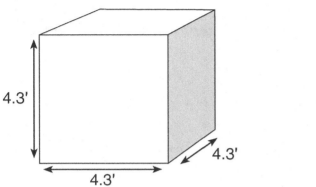

4.3'

4.3'

4.3'

Volume = _____

7. How much liquid can this oil tank store?

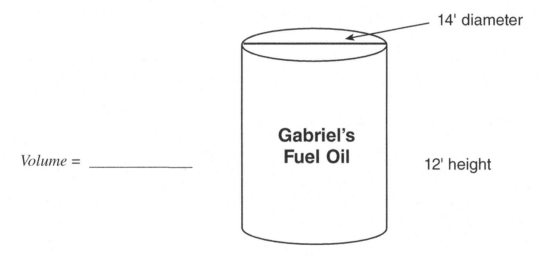

14' diameter

Gabriel's
Fuel Oil

12' height

Volume = _____

8. What is the volume of this cube?

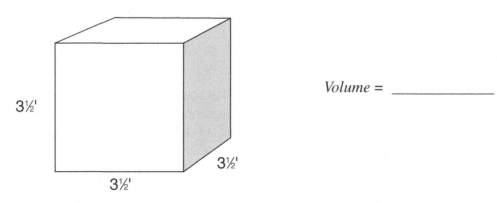

3½'

3½'

3½'

Volume = _____

The students at Wood Hill Elementary were surprised one day in gym class when the coach handed out a math test.

"What's going on?" they asked.

"Good athletes have to be good students, too," said the coach. "You don't want to be disqualified from a team because of poor grades. Answer these questions." He gave them each sheet of paper.

1. The volleyball net is 1 m wide and 9.50 m long. What are the perimeter and the area of the net?
   perimeter = _____ area = _____

2. The service area in volleyball is 3 m long and 3 m wide.

   What is the perimeter and the area of the service area? perimeter = _____
   area = _____

3. The volleyball court is 18 m long and 9 m wide. It is divided into two halves. What are the perimeter and the area of each half? perimeter = _____ area = _____

4. Tiffany runs 3 times around the volleyball court. How far does she run? _____

5. The badminton net is 0.76 m wide and 6.10 m long. What are the perimeter and area of the net?
   perimeter = _____ area = _____

6. The badminton net is 1.55 m high (1 m = 100 cm). What is its height in centimeters?
   _____

7. The badminton court is 13.40 m long and 6.10 m wide. It is divided into two halves. What is the perimeter of each half? _____ How many square meters of material would it take to cover one half? _____

8. Dan runs 5 times around the badminton court. How far does he run? _____

Ira has agreed to do a project for his father in exchange for a new snowboard this winter. Ira needs to paint the garden shed in his backyard. His father needs to buy the paint for the shed and has asked Ira to measure the size of each wall to determine the amount of paint he should purchase. There are four walls to the shed.

9. After measuring the walls, Ira has determined that each wall is 7 feet high and 12 feet long. What is the area of each wall? _____

10. What is the total area of the walls around the shed? _____

11. If a quart of paint covers 100 square feet, how many quarts of paint must Ira's father purchase?
    _____

12. Dan O'Leary has decided to plant a garden. He wants to make it 10.1 m long and 4.2 m wide. However, in order to keep the rabbits out, Dan needs a fence surrounding the garden. He decides to make the fence 11.2 m long and 5.0 m wide. What is the area between the fence and the garden? _____

    (**Hint:** Find the area for the garden. Then, find the area of the space surrounded by the fence.)

> The rod is an old unit of measurement of length. A rod is 16 1/2 feet long. A square rod is a square plot of ground. Each side of the plot is 16 1/2 feet long. An acre is 160 square rods.

13. How many square feet are in one acre? _____

14. How many square yards are in one acre? _____

15. A football field is 160 feet wide and 300 feet from goal line to goal line. What is the area of the football field in acres? (round to the nearest hundredth) _____

16. Mr. Anderson is a farmer. He has a 300-acre field. He expects to harvest about 225 bushels of corn per acre. A bushel of corn weighs about 56 pounds. How many pounds of corn would Tom get from his field? _____

> Mr. Peterson is a math teacher. Dinner at his house is unusual. One night, after a pizza was delivered, he posed the following questions to his hungry family. "Before we eat this delicious pizza, let's answer a few interesting questions," he said. Everyone groaned. "The radius of a regular pizza is 40 cm. Now, listen closely to my questions."

17. Find the area and the circumference of the pizza.
    area = _____ circumference = _____

18. If an ant walked 1 cm in 4 seconds, how long would it take for the ant to walk the circumference? _____

19. Repeat question #18 assuming the radius of the pizza is increased by 25%. Find the following measurements:

    radius = _____   area = _____

    circumference = _____   ant's time = _____

20. Repeat question #18 assuming the radius of the pizza is decreased by 25%. Find the following measurements:

    radius = _____   area = _____

    circumference = _____   ant's time = _____

11 ▸ Brain Teasers •••••••••••• Carpenters and Pyramids

Directions: Answer these brain teaser questions.

1. Four strips of paneling 40 cm long and 4 cm wide are arranged to form a square, like a picture frame. (**Note:** The ends of the strip of paneling will overlap.)

   What is the area of the inner square in square cm? _____

It's "Challenge Day" in Mr. Peterson's math class. "Take out a sheet of paper," he says. "Now, draw a 2 cm x 2 cm square. Listen closely.

---

2. What is the equation for finding the perimeter of a square that is twice the size of the original square? _____

3. What is the equation for finding the perimeter of a square that is four times the size of the original square? _____

4. What is the equation for finding the area of a square that is twice the size of the original square? _____

5. What is the equation for finding the area of a square that is four times the size of the original square? _____

6. In the following diagram of the front view of the Great Pyramid, the measure of ∠ PRQ is 120° degrees, and the measure of ∠ PST is 110° degrees.

   What is the measure of ∠ RPS in degrees? _____

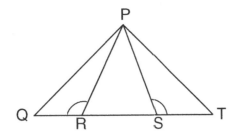

(**Hint:** The sum of the angles in a triangle is 180 degrees. A straight line is 180 degrees. Use the known angles to find the unknown angles. See Unit 3 on supplementary angles to help you solve the problem.)

7. One side of square *B* is four times the length of one side of square *A*. How many times greater is the area of square *B* than the area of square *A*? _____

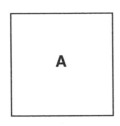

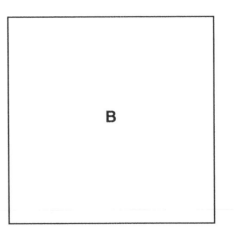

8. Two carpenters decided to design desks for students at James Hart Junior High. The dimensions of the desks are as shown. How much wood in cm² would they need for 30 desks? _____

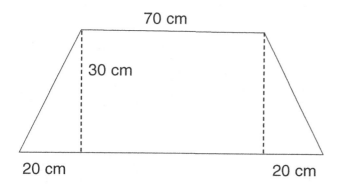

(**Hint:** What is the area of one desk? Find the area of each part and add all the areas to find the total area. If there are 30 desks, how much wood in square centimeters is needed?)

9. Do these parallelograms have the same area? How do you know? _____

_____

_____

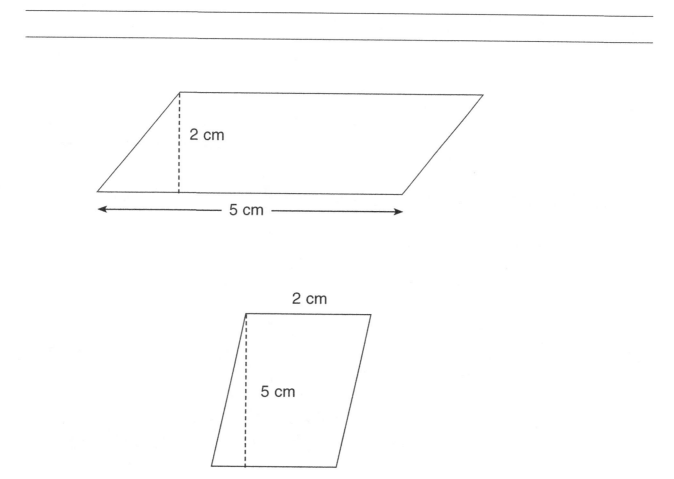

(**Hint:** Review the formula for finding the area of a parallelogram.)

Directions: Using drawing tools in a word-processing program such as *Microsoft Word®* or *AppleWorks®*, create your own geometric artwork. (**Note:** The following information explains the steps involved in creating your artwork using *Microsoft Word*, but the steps can be modified for use with any comparable software.)

1. Open a new *Word* document.

2. Click on the **Center** button on the **Formatting Toolbar**. Choose a large font size (26 to 36 points). Type a title for your artwork.

3. From the **INSERT** menu, choose **Pictures**, then **AutoShapes** from the drop-down menu.

4. In the **AutoShapes** window, choose the second option, **Basic Shapes**. Select the first shape in the pop-up window that you would like to use.

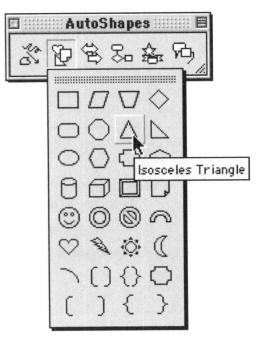

5. Click under the title to insert the shape that you have selected into any place on your new document. To use this shape more than once, pull down the **EDIT** menu with the shape still selected. Select **Copy**, then **Paste**. A copy of the shape you have selected will appear on top of the original. Move the copy to a new location on your document. Select **Paste** again as needed if you want the shape repeated.

6. Repeat the necessary steps to select different shapes to create your picture. Make sure to save your work often while creating your picture. Try to use different shapes and place shapes within shapes.

7. Print your artwork after you have completed the assignment. Color or decorate your picture and hang it up on the classroom bulletin board.

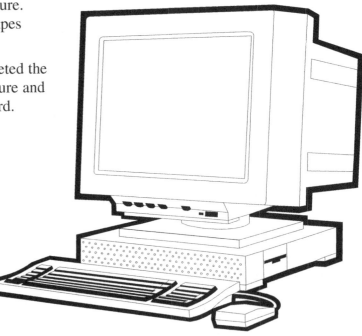

Examples of Geometric Artwork

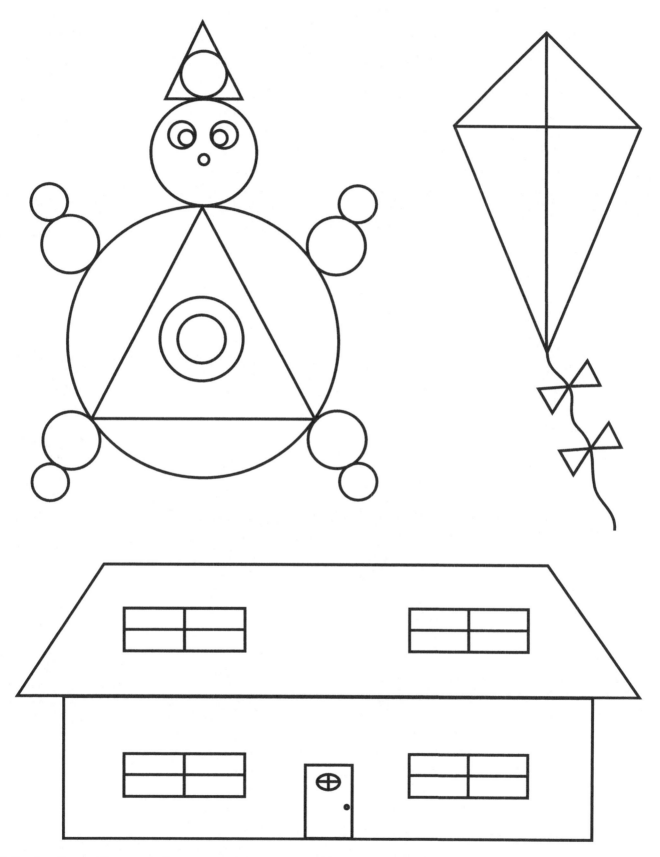

Pages 7 and 8
1. d
2. g
3. b
4. h
5. b
6. e
7. b
8. e
9. a
10. f
11. c
12. g
13. d
14. f

Pages 12 and 13
1. b
2. f
3. a
4. f
5. b
6. g
7. d
8. e
9. b
10. e
11. c
12. h

Page 17
1. 80°
2. 80°
3. 100°
4. 15°
5. ∠ g
6. ∠ f
7. 110°
8. 70°
9. 70°
10. 180°
11. 360°
12. 30°
13. 30°
14. 150°
15. 30°

Pages 20 and 21
1. radius
2. diameter
3. chord
4. circumference
5. 4 ft.
6. 6 in.
7. 9 ft.
8. 8½ in.
9. 1¾ in.
10. 110 ft.
11. 20.41 miles
12. 5½ yds.
13. 452.16 ft.²
14. 615.44 in.²
15. 314 ft.²

Page 25
1. acute
2. equilateral
3. right
4. isosceles
5. obtuse
6. scalene
7. acute
8. isosceles
9. acute
10. scalene
11. acute
12. equilateral

Page 29
1. 60°
2. acute and scalene
3. 60°
4. acute and equilateral
5. ∠ D = 55°
   ∠ F = 55°
6. 50°
7. c = 2.5"
8. b = 12'

Pages 32 and 33
1. parallelogram
2. trapezoid
3. rhombus
4. rectangle
5. trapezoid

6. parallelogram
7. 120 ft.
8. 36 ft.
9. 2.75 ft.
10. 7 ft.
11. 45 ft.
12. 14 ft.

Pages 36 and 37
1. 120 ft.²
2. 48 ft.²
3. 400 yds.²
4. 110.25 in.², 176 in.²
5. 40 ft.²
6. 14.625 ft.²
7. 12 ft.²
8. 6 in.²
9. 6 ft.²
10. 21.85 ft.²
11. 37.1 ft.²
12. 117 in.²

Pages 40 and 41
1. 385 in.³
2. 125 in.³
3. 2,154 in.³
4. 565.2 in.³
5. 400 ft.³
6. 79.507 ft.³
7. 1,846.32 ft.³
8. 42⅞ ft.³ or 42.875 ft.³

Pages 42 and 43
1. 21 m; 9.5 m²
2. 12 m; 9 m²
3. 36 m; 81 m²
4. 162 m
5. 13.72 m; 4.64 m²
6. 155 cm
7. 25.6 m; 40.87 m²
8. 195 m
9. 84 ft.²
10. 336 ft.²
11. 4 quarts
12. 13.58 m²
13. 43,560 ft.²
14. 4,840 yards²
15. 1.10 acres

16. 3,780,000 pounds
17. A = 5,024 cm²
    C = 251 cm
18. 16.75 minutes
19. r = 50 cm
    A = 7,850 cm²
    C = 314 cm
    time = 20.93 min
20. r = 30 cm
    A = 2,826 cm²
    C = 188.4 cm
    time = 12.56 min

Pages 44 and 45
1. 32 cm² = 1,024 cm²
2. P = 2(4s) = 16 cm
3. P = 4(4s) = 32 cm
4. A = 4(1 x w) = 16 cm²
5. A = 16(1 x w) = 64 cm²
6. 50°
7. Let side of square A = 1 cm

   Let the side of square B = 4 cm

   Area square A = 1 cm

   Area square B = 16 cm

   The area of square B is 16 times greater than the area of square A.
8. Area of rectangle = 70 cm x 30 cm = 2,100 cm²

   2,100 cm² + 600 cm² = 2,700 cm²

   30 x 2,700 cm² = 81,000 cm² of wood
9. Yes, they have the same area. Since you multiply the base and height, and these two parallelograms use the same numbers, so it doesn't matter which is the base and which is the height.

Made in the USA
Las Vegas, NV
08 February 2022

43434786R00031